Be a Zillionaire

The Young Zillionaire's Guide to

Taxation and Government Spending

Marie Bussing-Burks

the rosen publishing group's
rosen
central

Published in 2000 by The Rosen Publishing Group, Inc.
29 East 21st Street, New York, NY 10010

Library of Congress Cataloging-in-Publication Data

Bussing-Burks, Marie.
    The young zillionaire's guide to taxation and government spending / Marie Bussing-Burks.
        p.   cm. — (Be a zillionaire)
    Includes bibliographical references and index.
    ISBN 0-8239-3262-1
    1. Taxation—United States. 2. United States—Appropriations and expenditures. 3. Debts, Public—United States. I. Title. II. Series.
    HJ2362 .B87 2000
    336.73—dc21   99-086074

Manufactured in the United States of America

TABLE OF CONTENTS

The Government Spends Big

We need the government because it provides us with important goods and services—the kinds of goods and services that individuals and private companies do not have the resources to provide. You use government goods and services every day. The highways, public education systems, and the national defense are all government functions. Even your local subway or city bus system is a government service. Your grandparents are happy to get their monthly Social Security retirement check, and they have the government to thank for that, too.

For these reasons, the government is a big spender. About one-third of all the money disbursed in the United States every year is spent by the government. There are actually three levels of government: federal, state, and local. The spending habits of each are quite different, although all levels provide goods and services that are impractical for individuals or businesses to supply.

What Do Governments Buy?

The United States federal government spent around $1.8 trillion in 1999. Providing Social Security checks to retirees is the biggest expense. National defense is next in line. Third is income security: that is, welfare payments and unemployment compensation. Other large expenses on the federal level include net interest (the fee the government must pay when it borrows money), Medicare (a medical plan to help seniors), and health programs. Foreign aid and veterans' benefits are among the many smaller spending items grouped in the "other" category.

In the following chart, outlays of state and local governments are grouped together. State and local governments spend mainly on community services. In 1999 they spent approximately $1 trillion. A survey by

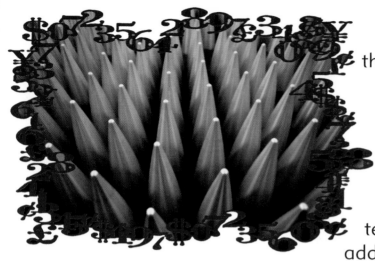

the United States Bureau of the Census shows that education is the biggest expense. School buildings, supplies, and teachers' salaries all add up. The next large items are public welfare, which helps low-income people, and the state highway system. In the "other" category we find expenditures for public transportation and police protection.

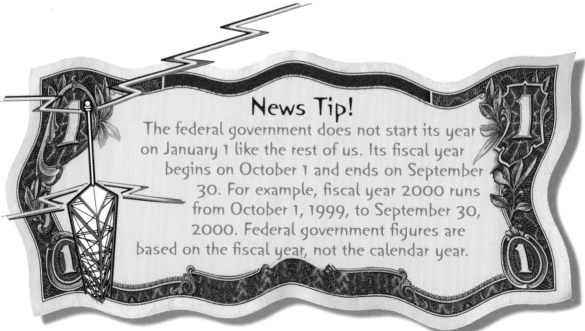

News Tip!

The federal government does not start its year on January 1 like the rest of us. Its fiscal year begins on October 1 and ends on September 30. For example, fiscal year 2000 runs from October 1, 1999, to September 30, 2000. Federal government figures are based on the fiscal year, not the calendar year.

Federal Spending Compared to State and Local Spending

Federal Spending (1999 estimates)

Social Security 23%
National Defense 16%
Income Security 14%
Net Interest 13%
Medicare 12%
Health Programs 8%
Other 14%

State and Local Spending (1995-96)

Education 33%
Public Welfare 17%
Highways 7%
Other 43%

Source: Economic Report to the President, U.S. Bureau of the Census

Now you know an important lesson about economic activity in the United States. Not all spending is carried on by individuals and businesses. Much commerce is conducted by federal, state, and local governments. The government is an important provider of many essential goods and services that we use every day.

Where Does the Money Come From?

We know that the government spends a lot. But where does it get all that money? Most government spending is financed by taxes. As we will see, the government collects taxes in a number of ways. And, yes, the federal government collects taxes differently than state and local governments.

Federal Government Revenue

The federal government collected over $1.9 trillion in taxes in 1999. The chart that follows shows that the largest source of revenue for the federal government comes from personal, individual income taxes. Every April 15, your father, mother, uncle, aunt, and grandparents pay a part of the income they earned during the prior year to the Internal Revenue Service. It is a legal obligation, if you earn

over a certain base level of
income. Social Security payroll taxes are the second
biggest source of federal
income. Everyone who
works must give a portion of
his or her paycheck to the
Social Security fund. When
workers retire, the money is
paid back to them in the
form of monthly retirement
checks. Corporate income
tax is the next big source of
revenue. Businesses must
pay a share of their profits
to the federal government.

Other revenue items include excise taxes on gasoline, alco-
hol and cigarettes, and custom duties on imported goods.

State and Local Revenue

State and local governments collect a great deal of money
from taxes, around $1.2 trillion in 1999. As the chart
shows, sales tax is the largest category. Most state governments collect a sales tax on goods and services sold in the
state. Secondly, the federal government transfers some of
its income to state and local governments to spend. Local
governments also benefit from the third greatest revenue
source: property taxes. Property taxes are payments based

on the value of your home or land. Fourth and fifth, respectively, are the income taxes individuals and businesses pay to state and local governments. Utility taxes and income from invested funds from employee pensions are some of the revenue sources in the "other" category.

Federal Revenue Compared to State and Local Revenue

Federal Revenue (1999 estimates)

Personal Income Taxes 47%
Social Security Payroll Taxes 34%
Corporate Income Taxes 11%
Other 8%

State and Local Revenue (1995-96)

Sales Tax 24%
Federal Transfers 20%
Property Taxes 19%
Individual Income Taxes 16%
Corporate Income Taxes 3%
Other 18%

Source: Economic Report to the President, U.S. Bureau of the Census

How Is Tax Calculated?

As you can see, there are different types of taxes. No matter what level of government collects the tax, all taxes can be described in three different ways—progressive, proportional, or regressive.

Progressive Taxation

The federal tax on individuals and businesses is an example of a progressive tax. The more money a person or firm makes, the greater the percentage paid in taxes. For example, current personal income tax rates start at 15 percent for moderate-income individuals and rise to nearly 40 percent for high-income earners.

The tax rates are progressive because high-income earners pay a larger percentage in taxes. Those who think that a progressive tax is a good idea believe that people and businesses with more money should pay a proportionally greater amount. Others argue that this is unfair to those people and businesses who work hard and earn a lot.

Proportional Taxation

A proportional tax rate is one that remains the same, regardless of the size of one's income. A 4 percent proportional tax on an income of $10,000 would be $400. If you made $100,000, you would still pay only 4 percent, so your bill would be $4,000. Only a few states tax individuals at a proportional rate. Pennsylvania uses a proportional income tax rate of 2.8 percent. Most states have progressive income tax rates.

Some individuals like this kind of tax because it treats everyone equally. Everyone has the same tax rate. Many who favor proportional taxes think that it would be fairer and easier than our complex federal progressive tax.

Regressive Taxation

Most taxes, other than income taxes, are regressive. With a regressive tax, the higher the income, the smaller the percentage of income paid as taxes. Most states charge sales taxes, which are regressive in relation to income. Sales taxes are calculated as a percentage of the selling price of goods and services. State sales taxes vary a great deal. Examples include a 3 percent sales tax in Colorado and a 6 percent sales tax in Florida.

Let's look at an example in which the state sales tax is 5 percent. The Johnson family makes $50,000 a year

Johnsons

Earn: $50,000/year
Spend: $20,000/year
Tax: $1,000
=1/50th total income

and spends $20,000 for living expenses, while the Wilson family makes $20,000 and spends their entire income on necessities. Both the Johnsons and the Wilsons pay $1,000 in tax (5 percent of $20,000). A closer look shows that the Johnsons pay only 1/50th of their total income in sales tax, while the Wilsons pay 1/20th of their total income in sales tax.

Lower income earning families like the Wilsons generally spend a greater fraction of their earnings on sales tax. Lower income families are therefore burdened by regressive taxes. Those who argue against a regressive tax say that it is unfair to the poor because it requires them to spend a larger portion of their income on basic needs.

Wilsons

Earn: $20,000/year
Spend: $20,000/year
Tax: $1,000
=1/20th total income

The major problem in organizing a fair tax system is determining who will pay the tax. Our government has decided that a just system requires a combination of these three forms of taxes.

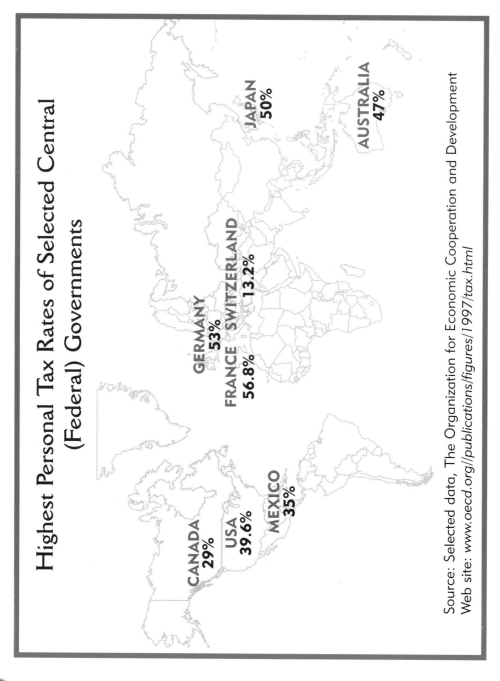

Highest Personal Tax Rates of Selected Central (Federal) Governments

CANADA 29%

USA 39.6%

MEXICO 35%

GERMANY 53%

FRANCE 56.8%

SWITZERLAND 13.2%

JAPAN 50%

AUSTRALIA 47%

Source: Selected data, The Organization for Economic Cooperation and Development
Web site: www.oecd.org//publications/figures/1997/tax.html

14

Completing the Picture

The government operates like a family. If a family spends more than it earns, it must borrow to make up the difference. So, too, must the government borrow. It could simply print all the money it needed, but that would lead to serious economic problems, such as inflation. To measure how well the government is managing its budget, and if it needs to borrow, is fairly simple. Add up all the tax money collected during the year and subtract all the money the government has spent during the year.

Types of Budgets

If taxes equal government spending, the budget is balanced. It is unusual for a government to have an exactly balanced budget. More commonly, budgets are in deficit or surplus. If the government spends

less than it collects, the budget has a surplus; if it spends more than it collects, the budget has a deficit.

People are concerned about a budget deficit because the government must borrow money to pay for its excess spending. The government is then in debt and must pay back what it owes with interest. You as a taxpayer are responsible for and will ultimately have to pay that debt. Budget surpluses, on the other hand, are generally viewed favorably. The government appears to be managing its money properly, and taxes may even be reduced.

State and local governments do a pretty good job of balancing their budgets each year. As a matter of fact, state and local governments throughout the U.S., as a group, usually run a small surplus every year. State and local governments enjoyed an estimated $169 billion surplus in 1999. They are in good shape. We will concentrate instead on the federal government, because it struggles to balance its budget. In 1998 the federal government finally got a grip on its spending habits.

That year it had its first surplus since 1969.

The Federal Budget

Let's take a closer look at two important years: 1997, when the federal government still ran a deficit, and 1998, when a surplus budget appeared.

Year	Taxes	Government Spending	Budget
1997	$1,579,300,000,000	$1,601,200,000,000	= –$21.9 Billion
1998	$1,721,800,000,000	$1,652,600,000,000	= +$69.2 Billion

Sure enough, in 1997 the federal government had a deficit. The government spent $21.9 billion more than it collected in taxes. But in 1998 the government showed a surplus by collecting $69.2 billion more than it spent. In 1999 the government had a $122.7 billion surplus. Surplus budgets are projected to follow. Sounds good. Then what is all the fuss about? Why are so many people complaining about the federal government's budget? The answer is debt.

Just because the government runs a budget surplus in one year, it cannot forget about all those years that it had to borrow money. Hey, when you borrow, you have to pay it back. The government does, too. The debt is calculated by adding up all the previous annual deficits and subtracting any surpluses. And are you ready for the total? Drum roll, please! The national debt had reached a total of $5.6 trillion by 1999! It will take a lot of surpluses to pay down such a large debt.

There are several official names for the U.S. debt of $5.6 trillion: the gross federal debt, the gross national debt, or the gross debt. Gross here doesn't mean ugly or uncool debt; it simply means the total debt.

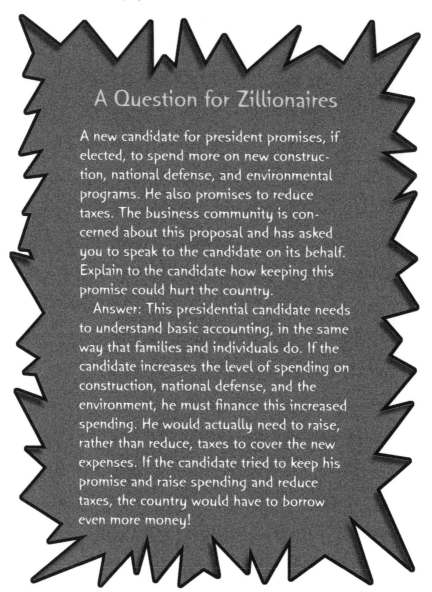

A Question for Zillionaires

A new candidate for president promises, if elected, to spend more on new construction, national defense, and environmental programs. He also promises to reduce taxes. The business community is concerned about this proposal and has asked you to speak to the candidate on its behalf. Explain to the candidate how keeping this promise could hurt the country.

Answer: This presidential candidate needs to understand basic accounting, in the same way that families and individuals do. If the candidate increases the level of spending on construction, national defense, and the environment, he must finance this increased spending. He would actually need to raise, rather than reduce, taxes to cover the new expenses. If the candidate tried to keep his promise and raise spending and reduce taxes, the country would have to borrow even more money!

How Big Is the Debt?

The huge national debt is not a new story. The United States first went into debt in 1790, when it assumed the Revolutionary War obligations of the Continental Congress. The debt was just over $75 million at the end of 1790. The first major increase in government debt occurred during World War II, when it rose from $40 billion to $279 billion. Our chance to reduce the debt was hindered by the Korean War in the early 1950s. The Vietnam War, which began in the mid-1960s, enlarged the debt even further. Early on, people were not concerned about the debt if it arose because of spending on war efforts.

In recent years, the United States has not faced a major war crisis. Still, the country's debt has grown rapidly. By 1980 the debt stood at $1 trillion. Today the debt of $5.6 trillion is drawing a lot of attention. Politicians and the public are beginning to ask, "Does this large debt present a problem?"

Problems with the Rising Debt

There are many opinions about the rising debt. Let's review four concerns that economists and others have about the national debt.

Rise in Interest Rates

When the U.S. government borrows large amounts of funds, it increases the competition for borrowed money. This increased demand tends to raise interest rates slightly. Most economists say that this is not a big concern because the increase in interest rates is almost unnoticeable. But should the debt continue to increase. . .

Impact on Future Generations

Some people argue that a rising debt burdens future generations, who must pay back the debt. Because the United States government is going to continue in business, it is not necessary to repay the entire debt at any one time. Governments, in theory, never fail to pay what they owe. Future generations could continue borrowing. Future generations must, at least, tax themselves to pay the interest charges. The people who own the debt will receive those interest payments as income.

Interest Charges

Another concern is that as the debt increases, interest payments may become a substantial portion of the federal government's spending package. This would force the government to reduce spending on other important goods and services. Economists are worried about the large amount of money being used just to pay interest.

A Limited Quantity of Credit

The government may have to borrow money to repay the debt. Businesses also borrow funds to build new factories, buy machinery, and hire more workers. Government borrowing takes away funds that would have been used by businesses. An increase in the debt results in more government goods at the expense of business-produced goods.

This is a big concern for those who prefer a small government. Many economists agree that it is one of the key disadvantages of a rising debt.

Advantages

Let's not, however, forget about the benefits that occur because of the high debt. The government has provided us with many essential goods and services, and through massive spending it has lifted our economy out of depression and recession many times. The bonds and securities that the government uses to finance the debt provide many investors with secure savings instruments.

How to Spend Money You Don't Have

We know that the U.S. government owes $5.6 trillion. But where did the government borrow that much? Who would lend the federal government trillions of dollars? What are the secure savings instruments the government uses to borrow?

The U.S. government has financed the debt by selling bonds and securities. About $2 trillion of the debt is held by government agencies, like the Social Security Administration, which invests its surplus in bonds and securities. The federal government borrows the other $3.6 trillion, or the net debt, from individuals, businesses, banking institutions, and foreigners. Fortunately, savers view government bonds and securities as excellent investments because they are a safe way to store money. The federal government always pays investors back. Government bonds and securities offer a good interest rate for the use of loaned money. There are four main types of bonds and securities sold by the U.S. Treasury: Treasury bills, Treasury notes, Treasury bonds, and savings bonds.

Treasury Bills
Treasury bills are short-term securities that mature, that is, come due for payment, in one year or less. These securities are high-priced—the minimum amount is $10,000. The Treasury bill interest rate is a widely watched rate. Many business and consumer loans are based on the Treasury bill rate. Often these loans are a few points higher than the Treasury rate and vary with that rate.

Treasury Notes
Treasury notes are intermediate federal securities with maturities of from one to ten years. Notes range from $1,000 to $5,000. Interest rates for notes are slightly

higher than for bills. Investors wait longer to get their money back, so they demand a higher interest rate.

Treasury Bonds

Treasury bonds are issued in units of $1,000. Maturities range from ten to thirty years. Interest rates for Treasury bonds are generally higher than rates for bills or notes. Investors loan the federal government money for a long time when they buy bonds. In turn, investors expect a higher interest rate.

Savings Bonds

United States savings bonds are issued in amounts ranging from $50 to $10,000. Because they are more reasonably priced, many consumers enjoy investing in savings bonds. They also make great gifts for birthdays, anniversaries, and graduations. Ask Mom and Dad if you have received any savings bonds. If you own a bond, you own a piece of the debt. Treasury bills, notes, and bonds are marketable securities. You can trade the securities with other investors before they mature. That way, if needed, you can get your money back before the issue matures. Savings bonds are nonmarketable. You can't trade them with other investors, but you can cash them in at your local banking institution.

The World Market for U.S. Debt

Luckily, because U.S. bonds and securities have so many great features, they are easy for the government to sell.

Even businesses and companies outside the United States like our government securities and bonds. Foreign individuals and businesses hold approximately 23 percent of the U.S. debt. The other part is held internally.

When debt is internal, the United States essentially owes the money to itself—an American business, banking institution, or government agency. The large percentage of debt that is owed to foreigners concerns some economists. This is a lot of money that must be paid back by Americans to people and businesses outside of the U.S. economy. That money ends up in other countries, adding to their economic growth, not ours.

Reducing the Debt

Government estimates suggest we are headed for years of modest surplus budgets. This is great news: The country is headed in a positive direction. But we still have a $5.6 trillion debt. The Treasury is using the annual surpluses to pay down the net debt. But we have a long way to go. So despite some politicians' optimistic predictions that the country will soon be debt-free, it is highly unlikely that the debt is going away anytime soon.

Questions for Zillionaires

1. During fiscal year 1999, the average debt increase each day was . . .
   A. $356
   B. $356 million
   C. $356 trillion

2. Today, each United States citizen's share of the debt is near . . .
   A. $21
   B. $21,000
   C. $21 million

3. In 1800, the per person share of the U.S. debt was slightly more than . . .
   A. $15
   B. $15,000
   C. $15 million

4. The current statutory debt limit—the maximum amount of government securities that can legally be outstanding at any time—is . . .
   A. $5.95 million
   B. $5.95 billion
   C. $5.95 trillion
   (When the limit is reached, the president and Congress must enact a new law to increase the limit.)

5. Government estimates predict by 2004 a debt of . . .
   A. $0
   B. $5.9 million
   C. $5.9 trillion

Answers: 1(B), 2(B), 3(A), 4(B), and 5(C).

Changing Taxes and Government Spending

We know that the government provides us with goods and services. The government imposes taxes to raise money to pay for these goods and services. But wait. There is another reason that the government might want to tax and spend. It is called fiscal policy.

Fiscal Policy

Fiscal policy is the government's plan for taxing and spending for the purpose of controlling the economy and its rate of expansion. It is designed to regulate the amount of spending by citizens and businesses by changing our available income. We currently spend around $9 trillion buying goods and services each year in the United States.

If the president and Congress feel that we should be spending more or less, they can organize a fiscal plan.

Contractionary Policy

What happens if people are spending too much money? Store owners won't be able to keep products on the shelves. They might even think they are not charging enough for their products and decide to raise prices. If workers begin to notice that store prices are rising, they will go to their bosses and ask for a raise. Hey, they need more money to buy those expensive items. And the spiral of wage and price increases continues. This is called inflation.

If the president and Congress feel that prices are rising too fast, they might use fiscal policy to dampen spending. Also called a contractionary policy, the plan would be to increase taxes or reduce government spending. Because the government is spending less, a tight policy reduces the amount of money in the economy available to purchase goods and services. Because taxes are increased, individuals and businesses have less money to spend on goods and services. This decreased spending ultimately decreases the demand for goods and services and brings down prices.

Expansionary Policy

The government might consider a different fiscal policy if the economy is not growing fast enough and there are not enough jobs. With an expansionary policy, the president and Congress call for increased government spending or reduced taxes. By spending more, the government pumps money into the economy and leaves individuals with more money to buy things like groceries, clothes, and new cars. Businesses are left with more money to buy raw materials, build factories, and invest in new equipment. This creates a demand for additional production, and the economy expands. By reducing taxes, the government is counting on individuals and businesses with more funds to spend the money on goods and services. If individuals and businesses decide to save the extra money from the tax reduction, it won't stimulate economic activity as the government intended.

John Maynard Keynes, the Fiscal Guy

Economist John Maynard Keynes (1883-1946) was born in Cambridge, England. In his famous text published in 1936, *The General Theory of Employment, Interest, and Money*, Keynes attempted to explain the widespread

John Maynard Keynes

unemployment during in the Great Depression. He said that it was the government's responsibility to maintain high employment by spending on public works programs. His followers, the Keynesians, called this "fiscal policy." They encouraged the government to spend and to decrease taxes to increase economic activity.

Much of the planned spending in the United States during President Roosevelt's "New Deal" administration was based on Keynesian economics. It was designed to increase economic growth. The administration spent several billion dollars on many programs and projects designed to put people to work. The programs did increase economic growth, as the New Deal gave millions of people jobs, and those people could then purchase more goods and services, stimulating businesses to produce more.

Problems with Fiscal Policy

It would be great if fiscal policy were that easy—just change government spending or taxes, and the economy runs perfectly. In reality there are several problems with fiscal policy.

The Size of the Debt

The thing about spending to increase economic growth is that the government cannot get the money it needs through taxes. If it did, whatever money it put into the economy with one hand, it would be taking away with the other hand. Keynesian policy depends upon deficit spending—that is, you have to spend money you don't have. You have to borrow the money. When you have an expansionary fiscal policy and increase government spending, you must add to the government's debt.

Fiscal Policy Works Slowly

Assume that the government feels that taxes or spending appropriations should be changed to produce a healthier economy. In a democracy like ours, with many competing interest groups, it can take months or years for a bill to pass through Congress. By the time a bill is passed, the economic situation may have changed. Some economists believe that the government can never get it right and only makes things worse.

Knowing What to Do

We may all agree that the economy is not doing well, but the problem is knowing exactly how to fix it. Even economists can't always agree. To make it even more complicated, sometimes the economic data can be unclear. One government number might suggest that the economy is going strong, while another hints that we are headed for trouble.

Some fiscal policy is automatic. Automatic fiscal policy does not require congressional legislation. For example, economic activity falls during a recession because people don't work as much. The government then

Learning More
The job of the Office of Management and Budget is to help the president prepare the federal budget. Log on to *http://www.whitehouse.gov/OMB/index.html* to view the current federal budget and historical budget data. A citizen's guide to the federal budget provides an excellent description on how the budget is prepared, a glossary of important budget terms, and a sneak peak at the president's plan to eliminate the debt.

pays more for unemployment insurance to those who don't have jobs. These people spend the money on groceries and other necessities of life, and economic activity is automatically energized.

Historical Measures

Because fiscal policy is so complicated, the president and Congress rarely and reluctantly take an active role in adjusting government spending and taxes. Let's look at some historical examples and see how it worked out.

Expansionary Policy

Early in 1963, President Kennedy told the country that we were doing well but that we had not reached maximum income and employment levels. Kennedy used deficit spending to spur economic activity. At the same time he requested a tax reduction on personal and corporate incomes. After Kennedy's death, President Johnson signed a historic tax reduction bill in February, 1964. Johnson asked Americans to spend the increase in their incomes that would result from the tax cut. Most economists concur that the Johnson-Kennedy tax cut was a moderately successful expansionary program.

Contractionary Policy

Early in 1991, President Bush signed into law a federal budget calling for tax increases, spending cuts, and other measures designed to reduce an expected increase in the debt over the next five years. Although government spending was not actually reduced very much, the previously planned increases were lowered. Economists identified the tax increases and spending cuts as a contractionary sign that eventually resulted in lower prices.

Fiscal Discipline

President Clinton's main economic goal has been debt reduction. The first major accomplishment of the president's second term was an agreement with the Republican Congress on how to reach a balanced budget. Despite large tax cuts, the balance was achieved by trimming $263 billion from federal spending over a five-year period. During Clinton's administration, the country reached its first surplus in nearly thirty years. Some refer to the administration's policy as one of fiscal discipline.

A Challenge for Zillionaires

It is the year 2020, and you are an influential member of Congress. The president has informed Congress that the country's output of $38 trillion is just not high enough. The president wants Congress to come up with a basic plan that would increase this figure significantly. Newer members of Congress are looking to you to provide leadership. They have never dealt with such complicated economic calculations. You tell them not to worry. The answer is quite simple if you know some basic economics. What do you say to the other members of Congress?

Answer: You remind the members that to increase economic activity the government must use an expansionary fiscal policy. By increasing government spending in areas such as the environment and national defense, the country certainly could increase economic activity. The government could also give businesses and individuals a tax break. But these businesses and individuals must spend the money in the economy. Otherwise the plan will backfire.

News Tip!

Want to add a big bang to the U.S. economy? Try a combination of increased government spending and decreased taxes. Spending in the economy will be vigorous!

Take Action!

Most people would agree that the government does a good job of providing goods and services. You may also think that the government has a pretty good handle on the budget. Or maybe you have some spending or taxing suggestions. Whatever your views, who couldn't use a little extra help? Just like people, the government can always benefit from new ideas. And who better to provide input than young citizens with a fresh outlook. If you would like to get involved in how the government spends, taxes, and manages its finances, here are some ideas to get you started.

Make a Donation

Generally the Treasury Department believes that people fulfill their financial duties to the government by abiding by the tax regulations. Any additional action, like a donation to help pay off the national debt, is purely voluntary.

Acting for the Secretary of the Treasury, the Bureau of Public Debt may accept a gift of money made under the condition that it be used to reduce the national debt. Individuals wishing to contribute may send a letter stating their wishes, enclosed with a donation, to the Bureau of Public Debt, Department G, Washington, D.C. 20239-0601. The check must be made payable to the Bureau of Public Debt.

As you can see from the chart on page 39, some Americans feel strongly about contributing. In recent years the Bureau of Public Debt has collected about $1 million each year. In 1994 nearly $21 million was donated to reduce the debt. It was a super spectacular year for debt contributions. Donating to the debt should be a joint activity under guidance from your parents. Or talk to your teacher. A class project to help pay off the debt is a great way to take action!

Encourage Adults to Vote

Have you ever heard an adult complain about the way government money is being spent? Or perhaps the complaint is about taxes. Voting is one way citizens can participate indirectly in important spending and tax legislation decisions. Encourage voting for local representatives like your mayor or city and town councillors. Don't forget your governor, state legislators, and state senators.

The president is our highest elected federal official.

The presidential election is held every four years. Even if it is not a presidential election, every election is an important one. Adults should vote at every opportunity. Important spending and taxing decisions are going on at every level of government. Let adults know they can have a say in the way the government taxes and spends by electing individuals who best represent their views.

Contact Government Officials

Maybe you think the federal government should spend more money on the poor, or less money should be allocated to international affairs. Perhaps you are interested in the way your state is going to spend its surplus this year. A new youth center in your city might be your local lobbying point. Let your views be heard!

Thanks to modern technology it is easy to contact your government officials. E-mail is a great way to quickly voice your concerns. The great thing is that most elected officials have easily located e-mail addresses. But don't forget that there is nothing like a good old-fashioned letter. Most officials will actually write you back!

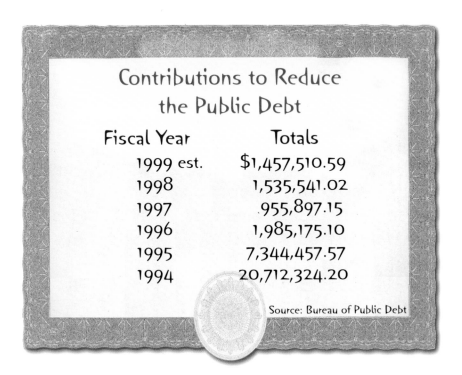

Contributions to Reduce the Public Debt

Fiscal Year	Totals
1999 est.	$1,457,510.59
1998	1,535,541.02
1997	955,897.15
1996	1,985,175.10
1995	7,344,457.57
1994	20,712,324.20

Source: Bureau of Public Debt

Speak Out!

Even though you can't vote yet, you can easily participate in government. Ask your parents if you can attend a local election debate or open forum. Don't be afraid to get involved. Does the candidate believe in a balanced budget, or is he or she a big spender? Find out! Ask candidates the following questions:

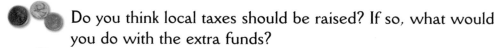 What changes will you make in the city (or state) budget if you are elected?

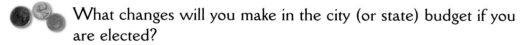 Do you think local taxes should be raised? If so, what would you do with the extra funds?

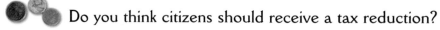 Do you think citizens should receive a tax reduction?

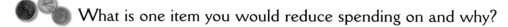 What is one item you would reduce spending on and why?

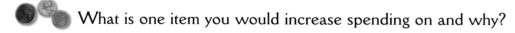 What is one item you would increase spending on and why?

Attend your local county and city council meetings. Here the discussion and voting will be on specific topics. The topic could be almost anything—making plans for a new subdivision of homes, buying equipment for the firehouse, or building a new town tennis court. Find out what is going on in your local area.

What's a Kid to Do?

It has been in all the papers—your local town council has proposed to tear down the historic community center.

40

It will be replaced with a new $5 million community center complex. There is so much concern over this proposal that the town council has scheduled an open forum for townspeople to share their views. What do you do?

Answer: You can do a lot. First of all, how do you feel about the proposal? Do you think it is a good use of funds? Then speak up. You might share with the council the things you and your friends would like to see in the center. Tell them that a pool, study room, and basketball court would be used a lot by people your age. Or maybe you think the new center is a bad idea. The historic community center is more than adequate for the town. The meeting rooms are used by young people and adults. The basketball court is old but spacious. Speak out! Mention all the fantastic things the town could do with $5 million— a shelter for the homeless, a community food bank, or a new park with outdoor play equipment. For $5 million, you may be able to provide all three.

Remember, the U.S. government is *your* government. And you are the leaders of tomorrow. Your actions will continue to ensure a strong, prosperous, and financially sound government.

GLOSSARY

Bureau of Public Debt   A bureau of the U.S. Treasury that borrows the funds necessary to operate the federal government and accounts for the resulting public debt. Its main function is to promote and sell U.S. savings bonds.

deficit   The annual excess of spending over revenues.

deficit spending   Federal government spending in excess of government tax revenue.

excise tax   An indirect tax levied on the purchase of certain goods, such as cigarettes or liquor.

fiscal policy   Government spending and taxing decisions that have been deliberately designed to expand or contract the economy.

gross national debt (GND)   The total value of all outstanding federal government bonds and securities.

interest rate   The rate paid for borrowing money.

Internal Revenue Service   The Internal Revenue Service (IRS) is the U.S. Treasury bureau charged with the administration of the tax laws passed by Congress. All federal tax returns are filed with this agency.

imports   Goods and services purchased by Americans from other countries.

net debt   The total value of all outstanding federal government bonds and securities minus those held by government agencies.

progressive tax   The higher the income, the greater the percentage of income paid in taxes.

proportional tax   A tax rates that stays the same, regardless of income level. Also called a flat tax.

regressive tax   The higher the income, the smaller the percentage of income paid in taxes.

surplus   The amount by which revenues exceed spending.

For More Information

Web Sites

Governors

http://www.nga.org
The National Governors' Association provides addresses and phone numbers to all state governors' offices.

Mayors

http://www.mayors.org
Go to this site and locate the "meet the mayors" icon. The United States Conference of Mayors provides access to your mayor and local government. Highlight your city to find e-mail addresses, mailing addresses, and a description of your local government.

President and Vice President

http://www.whitehouse.gov
A great Web site providing information on the inner workings of the White House. The site provides a quarterly newsletter, *Inside the White House*, just for kids. You can e-mail the president and vice president's offices with your concerns. Like to communicate the old-fashioned way? The White House mailing address is: 1600 Pennsylvania Avenue, Washington, D.C. 20500.

FOR MORE INFORMATION

Save Lab (Merrill Lynch)

http://www.plan.ml.com/family/kids/

The Senate and House of Representatives

http://www.congress.org
At this site, you can enter your zip code, and *presto!* You are given access to your senator and congressperson. Along with the official's e-mail and address information, their bill and voting record is provided.

Statistics Canada

http://www.statcan.ca
An excellent source of statistics on Canadian government finances, revenues, and federal spending.

Young Investor (Liberty Financial Company)

http://www.younginvestor.com/pick.shtml

Young Investor's Network (Salomon Smith Barney)

http://www.salomonsmithbarney.com/yin

FOR FURTHER READING

Feinberg, Barbara Silberdick. *Local Governments*. New York: Franklin Watts, 1993.

Feinberg, Barbara Silberdick. *The National Government*. New York: Franklin Watts, 1993.

Feinberg, Barbara Silberdick. *State Governments*. New York: Franklin Watts, 1993.

Hirsch, Charles, Samuel D. Woods, and Lila Summers. *Taxation: Paying for Government*. Austin, TX: Steck-Vaughn Company, 1993.

Keynes, John Maynard. *The General Theory of Employment, Interest, and Money*. Amherst, NY: Prometheus Books, 1997.

Pascoe, Elaine. *The Right to Vote*. Brookfield, CT: Millbrook Press, 1997.

Sandak, Cass R. *The National Debt*. New York: Twenty-First Century Books, 1996.

Weizmann, Daniel. *Take a Stand: Everything You Never Wanted to Know About Government*. Los Angeles, CA: Price Stern Sloan, 1996.

INDEX

About the Author

Marie Bussing-Burks holds a doctorate in economics and has taught the subject for ten years at the University of Southern Indiana. She lives in Newburgh, Indiana, with her husband, Barry, and her two daughters, Annemarie and Katy.

Photo Credits

Cover photo © Artville; pp. 5, 25, 28 © UNIPHOTO; pp. 6, 30, 38 and 40 © SuperStock; pp. 9, 10, 16, 21 by Maura Boruchow; p. 11 © Russ Wilson/SuperStock; p. 18 © Reuters/ Pool/Archive Photos; p. 20 © Anthony Potter Collection/Archive; p. 22 by Thaddeus Harden; p. 34 © Reuters/Remy Steinegger/Archive Photos.

Series Design

Law Alsobrook

Layout

Laura Murawski